# PROJECT ILPs
## Individualized Learning Plans
## for Life-Based Projects

**The Instructional Design Library**

*Volume 15*

# PROJECT ILPs
# Individualized Learning Plans
# for Life-Based Projects

Philip G. Kapfer
*University of Utah*
*Salt Lake City*

and

Miriam Bierbaum Kapfer
*University of Utah*
*Salt Lake City*

Danny G. Langdon
*Series Editor*

**Educational Technology Publications**
**Englewood Cliffs, New Jersey 07632**

**Library of Congress Cataloging in Publication Data**

Kapfer, Philip G
    Project ILPs.

    (The Instructional design library; v. no. 15)
    Bibliography: p.
    1. Individualized instruction. I. Kapfer,
Miriam B., joint author. II. Title. III. Series.
LB1031.K353    371.39'4    77-25409
ISBN 0-87778-119-2

Printed in the United States of America.

Library of Congress Catalog Card Number:
77-25409.

International Standard Book Number:
0-87778-119-2.

First Printing: February, 1978.
Second Printing: January, 1980.

To
Asahel D. Woodruff,
colleague and friend

# FOREWORD

Individualized Learning Plans (ILPs) are structures for giving students both the responsibility and the freedom to learn. The authors strike a careful but flexible balance between using ILPs for "learning how to learn" and for "learning subject matter content." They view both of these as being important while avoiding the fallacy of suggesting curriculum content that is suitable for all.

Project ILPs are ways of learning subject matter within the context of life-based pursuits, whether at school, at home, on the job, or at play. Inquiry ILPs, presented in the Kapfers' other volume in this series, are ways of learning subject matter either because of want (i.e., for curiosity satisfaction) or because of need (i.e., for making, producing, or achieving something). Although any one of the four ILP designs contained in the two Kapfer books may be used independently of the others, as a set they represent the major component of a highly integrated and systematic instructional system.

The Project ILP designs have a great deal of utility for teachers and students at every level. Project ILPs are basically simple designs that may be understood easily and applied in a variety of educational settings. They require only a "willingness to try" on the part of an individual teacher or a school staff. In this regard, I would direct your attention to the final paragraph in the "Outcomes" section of this book. You will find there an analogy that highlights a number of reasons for trying Project ILPs or, indeed, for trying any of the other designs in the Instructional Design Library. There is as much truth in this analogy as there are uses to be found for Project ILPs.

Danny G. Langdon
Series Editor

# PREFACE

This book presents the final two of four "Individualized Learning Plans" (ILPs) that have resulted from a decade of work on life-based education in the Life-Involvement Model (LIM) Project, initiated by Asahel D. Woodruff and currently co-directed by the authors.

The first two ILP designs, published as a separate volume in this series, are for the kinds of student goals that require inquiry-type learning. The present book contains two project-type ILP designs, for issue resolving and "product" making. Each of these has a place in the job of transforming conventional *subject-based* teaching-learning approaches into *life-based* education.

Project ILPs, while having interesting historical and theoretical antecedents, comprise a fresh new approach to teaching and learning. They are different because, rather than being isolated designs, they are part of a total approach to education that centers on learning as holistic, purposive, want-serving behavior.

Throughout this book the word "product" appears within quotation marks. This is an attempt to remind the reader that the word is being used in a very broad sense, that is, for anything produced by labor or effort. The important point is that "product" does not imply a mechanistic orientation.

The processes of issue resolving and "product" making, in our view, are pervasive in the lives of thinking, doing, working, playing, surviving people. Our task has been to create instructional designs that capitalize upon and offer structured practice in these two essential in-life behaviors. Thus, both types of Project ILPs are concerned with education that is behavior-oriented, life-relevant, individualized, and humanistic.

M.B.K.
P.G.K.

# CONTENTS

*xi*

# ABSTRACT

## PROJECT ILPs
### Individualized Learning Plans
### for Life-Based Projects

Two Individualized Learning Plans (ILPs) for life-based projects are presented—the Issue Project ILP and the Production Project ILP. These instructional designs are termed "life-based" because they emphasize processes that are engaged in, in one form or another, by most people throughout their lives. These processes are (1) choosing one's goals (or issue resolving), and (2) materializing one's goals (or "product" making).

The Issue Project ILP is designed to provide opportunities to practice the steps involved in resolving in-life issues in systematic and rational ways. The Production Project ILP is designed to encourage well-planned and motivationally sound production tasks in schools. Both types of Project ILPs integrate conceptual learning with its application, and both require the development of new competencies that are widely useful in life.

Project ILPs are appropriate and educationally sound for use in virtually all subject fields and at all instructional levels. Project ILPs may be used in classroom organizations that range from completely self-contained to highly department-alized. In any setting, however, student mastery of the processes involved is at least as important as student mastery of content. Student self-evaluation of both processes and "products" also is an essential part of the use of Project ILPs.

The processes emphasized in Project ILPs—issue resolving and "product" making—are the foundation for life-long learning, decision-making, productivity, and independence. As such, these processes are very important tools in a rapidly changing world.

# PROJECT ILPs
## Individualized Learning Plans
## for Life-Based Projects

# I.

# USE

Projects have been with us a long time. In fact, each and every person who has ever lived has engaged during his or her lifetime in one project after another, not to mention several projects simultaneously. Projects are not respectors of age; they are engaged in by pre-schoolers, by senior citizens, and by all those in between.

Projects are as pervasive as life itself. They are as divergent as human values, interests, and creativity will allow. They can be brief, lasting only a few minutes, or lengthy, taking years to accomplish. They involve phenomena as common as a loaf of bread or as other-worldly as King Solomon's temple to Yahweh. Projects may be individual or group efforts, they may be essentially unplanned or systematically designed, easily accomplished or acutely challenging, devoid of conceptual and motor learning for a given person or loaded with new understandings and skills, scholarly and academic or everyday and practical, personally want-serving or individually lacking in motivational appeal.

Projects exhibiting combinations of these and additional descriptors can be seen everywhere—at home, in school, out shopping, in church, on the job, in the hospital, on vacation, and wherever else people "do their thing." Projects are limited by only two factors—by the project doer's *ability* and by his or her *access* to whatever material and non-material resources are needed for accomplishing the project tasks.

In this book, we will focus on projects *within the school curriculum.** We will look at two unique instructional designs—two Individualized Learning Plans (ILPs)—for life-based projects. As presented in this book, Project ILPs may be thought of as the fourth and fifth "R's" of school. Project ILPs are the *R*EALITY and *R*ELEVANCE that give purpose to and that "carry" *required* learning. They are designed to serve distinctive educational purposes beginning in kindergarten and extending through the most advanced levels of general, professional, and technical education and training. For example, the particular subject matter content that is available to students by means of life-based Project ILPs is

---

*The earliest school-related use of the term "project" appears to have been by C.R. Richards in 1900 (Burton, 1929). Educators will quickly recall subsequent use of this term in connection with the early 20th century teaching approach known as the "project method" (Kilpatrick, 1918, 1921, and 1925).

Clearly, the two Individualized Learning Plans (ILPs) for life-based projects presented in this book are not a return to the "project method." The "project method" in its classic form involved four types of projects—(1) making or producing something, (2) enjoying an aesthetic experience, (3) solving a problem, and (4) obtaining skill or knowledge. Kilpatrick laid great stress on the motivational character of the project, that is, on the project as a unit of "whole-hearted purposeful activity." Others emphasized the additional requirement that the project be "carried to completion in its natural setting" (Charters, 1921). The four basic steps involved in the majority of Kilpatrick-type projects were purposing, planning, executing, and evaluating. Unfortunately, the appealing simplicity of these four steps does not often match the complexity of the kinds of tasks people do in life. What *can* be said is that both the "project method" and Project ILPs have similar psychological roots—in a humanistic theory of learning that considers the individual to be a purposive, developing organism whose knowledge, competence, values, and emotional stability are best developed through genuine perceptual experience with phenomena in the environment.

determined by the *need* for that content in the course of completing any chosen project. Project ILPs serve the additional educational purpose of familiarizing students with critical in-life learing-and-doing processes.

**Two Kinds of Project ILPs**

Two types of life-based projects will be illustrated and described in this book. The first is the "Issue Project ILP" and the second is the "Production Project ILP."

The Issue Project ILP requires the use of issues resolution processes for the purpose of rationally selecting a goal. For example:

What should be done about . . .
    (1)    Capital punishment?
    (2)    Child abuse?
    (3)    Protection of the environment?
    (4)    Poverty?
    (5)    My financial investments?
    (6)    Post-secondary education for me/you/them?
    (7)    Landscaping our school/community/home/business?
    (8)    Etc.

The two elements that are common to all of these issues are that they involve *values* and they have *alternative solutions* that differentially affect those values.

The Issue Project ILP may be developed whenever an issue is complex enough or important enough to require formal and rational resolution processes. The Issue Project ILP may be used in school by groups of students for the purpose of resolving an issue of common concern, or it may be used by individual students for resolving highly personal issues.

Once a given issue has been resolved through the selection of a goal, the various production processes employed in the Production Project ILP may then be used to facilitate goal attainment. The Production Project ILP may be used to produce a wide variety of possible "products" including examples from any of the following categories (adapted from Woodruff, 1973):

(1) Physical object
(2) Aesthetic object
(3) Developed idea
(4) Description of something
    (a) Anecdotal
    (b) Analytical
    (c) Evaluative
(5) Condition, arrangement, or set of circumstances
(6) Planned event
(7) Argument
(8) Proposal

By supplying specific examples to illustrate each of these categories, we can readily see the diversity of outcomes for which the Production Project ILP may be used, as follows: (1) *physical objects* such as plants, crystals, foods, and furniture; (2) *aesthetic objects* such as tapestries, jewelry, sculptures, and paintings; (3) *developed ideas* such as musical scores, short stories, and poems; (4) *descriptions* such as newspaper accounts of current events, legal descriptions of real estate, reviews of musical performances, and ecological impact studies; (5) *conditions, arrangements, or sets of circumstances* such as the terms for a purchase, plans for a cooperative child-care center, and entrance requirements for student clubs; (6) *planned events* such as committee meetings, class parties, ball games, programs, and vacation itineraries; (7) *arguments* such as preparing evidence for legal cases, preparing material for formal debates, and gathering scientific evidence on community issues; and (8) *proposals* such as thesis outlines, formal bids for construction jobs, and proposals for re-development of local landmarks. Obviously, such categories of "products" overlap repeatedly, but they do serve the purpose of suggesting endless ideas for challenging, content-loaded Production Project ILPs.

Production Project ILPs may be developed whenever systematic planning is needed for the achievement of a desired end. Such projects may be planned and carried out by individual students or by task groups. In the case of task groups, division of responsibility may occur both for planning and for performing the steps required for goal achievement.

Both the Issue and Production Project ILPs may be entirely teacher-planned and teacher-led or student-planned and student-conducted. These two possibilities should be thought of as the two end points of a continuum of student dependence/independence. The actual use of Project ILPs may involve, of course, any desired and educationally appropriate combination of teacher and student involvement. However, the fullest potential of the Project ILP *as a device for individualizing instruction* is reached in the student-constructed form of the ILP. Achievement of that full potential depends on the extent to which the student has learned the processes of *issue resolving* and *"product" making* that underlie each of the two kinds of Project ILPs. Therefore, a critically important teacher responsibility is to help the student to increasingly understand and practice the processes that are involved.

### Appropriate Content for Project ILPs

Subject matter content may be divided into two major categories for the purpose of life-based instructional designs: (1) content that consists of "end products," and (2) content that consists of components of those "end products."

*"End product" content.* This category of content is composed of all of those phenomena (objects and events) that people consider to be "ends" or potential goals.

Examples include material possessions such as homes, auto-
mobiles, clothing, and the like, as well as non-material
phenomena such as literature, music, the law, health, safety,
and friendship. The critical requirement of all phenomena
that are identified as being a part of this category is that such
phenomena must be perceived as being "products" *in
themselves,* for which students are willing to expend energy.

As people begin to specialize for particular occupations,
the "end products" they will produce using Project ILPs will
become more specialized also. For example, the beginning
student in restaurant food preparation may make one or
more basic salads and consider the completed items to be his
or her "product" at a given point in time. However, at
another time, as the student advances toward chef production and management skills, these salads may be thought of
as one of several parts of a larger "product," namely a
decorative cold buffet. Similarly, the medical student may
engage in a project in which the initial "product" may be the
differential diagnosis of liver disease for a patient whose chief
complaints are of jaundice, indigestion, and weight loss. As
the medical student progresses, he or she may identify as the
"end product" a total patient management plan, including a
diet high in protein and carbohydrates, abstinence from
alcohol, ample bed rest, and appropriate drug therapy.

*"Component" content.* This category of content includes
all those phenomena that are *components* of items in the first
category. For the student in food production, phenomena
such as fresh greens, other fresh and cooked vegetables, fresh
and cooked fruit, meat, fish, a wide variety of herbs,
specialized sauces and dressings, gelatines, aspics, an assort-
ment of ornamental molds, and so forth all are examples of
components of the "end product," namely salads in the
varying roles of appetizer, accompaniment to the entrée,
main course, or dessert. For the medical student who is

diagnosing the case of jaundice, phenomena such as bilirubin, bilirubin metabolism, liver anatomy, and the like are the "component" subject matter that must be functionally understood in order to achieve the "end product" of a diagnosis.

*Ways to identify curricular content.* Life-based education through the use of Project ILPs becomes a reality for students when teachers at every level make available outlines or indexes of possible "end products." The format and organization of such indexes are a matter of style and teacher-student preference. For young students, a pictorial index may be very helpful. For more mature students, verbal or symbolic lists in outline form or in flowcharts may be most efficient.

The procedure for developing such indexes is essentially one of *generating* increasingly specific categories until "end products" can be identified easily, followed by the more common process of *analyzing* single examples of "products" into their components. The details of these curriculum generation and analysis processes are beyond the scope of this book. However, two examples will serve our purposes here. In Figure 1, the very broad category of "economic institutions" was used as the starting point. Increasingly specific categories of phenomena were generated to the level of those just above the horizontal, dashed line. Then a single example—the Longview School "Write Right" Store—was analyzed to reveal phenomena that might comprise the curricular content in this area.

A second example, shown in Figure 2, is taken from medical education (Tolman and Kapfer, 1976). This figure also illustrates the processes of generation and analysis in identifying curricular content. In this figure, six broad categories of phenomena commonly acted upon by physicians were listed across the top, followed by an expansion of

*Figure 1*

## Economic Phenomena as Curricular Content:
## Generation Followed by Analysis

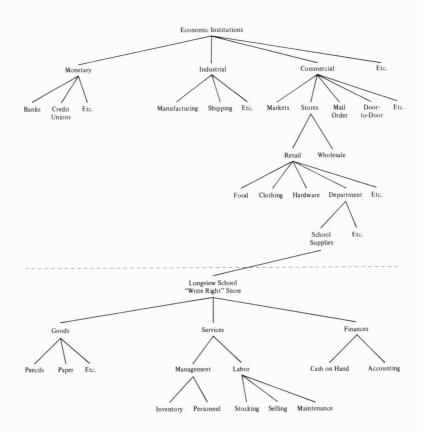

## Figure 2

## Medical Phenomena as Curricular Content: Generation Followed by Analysis

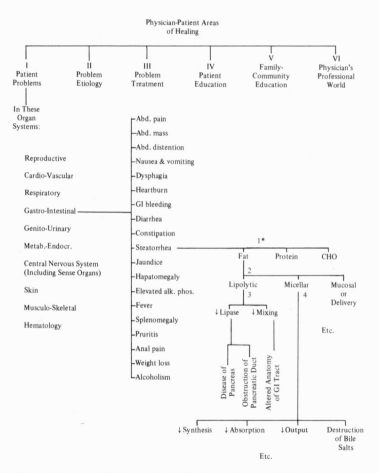

*In addition to the phenomena listed in the algorithm, the following curricular content also is involved:

(1)  History, stool-exam—gross and micro, fat balance.
(2)  Xylose test and small bowel x-ray, small bowel bx, pancreatic function test, BA test.
(3)  Abd. flat plate, pancreatic duct x-ray, UGI series.
(4)  Biliary tract x-ray, small bowel culture, liver biopsy.

the first category (patient problems) into ten organ systems. Categories of patient problems (or symptoms) then were generated from the gastro-intestinal organ system. One such problem, steatorrhea, then was analyzed to reveal some of the phenomena that must be understood in order to diagnose the cause of this problem. Assuming a diagnosis as the "end product," such phenomena are the "component" subject matter for medical student learning. A real or simulated patient with a single "problem" or a combination of "problems" would constitute the beginning of a series of Project ILPs. These projects could cycle through the six categories listed across the top of Figure 2.

The kind of curricular content that has been described and illustrated in this section is familiar to teachers, students, and parents alike. It is the "stuff" out of which textbooks are written. What may be less familiar is the way in which it is organized. A primary difference between the life-based approach to presenting content and other approaches is that the life-based approach exposes more clearly the specific *phenomena* with which the student must become competent. In addition, the student's attention is consistently focused on appropriate in-life and on-the-job uses for that content.

### When to Use Formally Prepared
### Project ILPs

Many Project ILPs should be written, step by step, in a rather formal fashion. Others probably will proceed as smoothly in a less detailed and largely oral mode. Critical factors in this decision include the age, academic level, purposes, interests, and independence level of the learner, as well as the classroom setting and predilections of the teacher. In any case, formal use of either of the Project ILP designs, whether pre-constructed by the teacher or developed and written by the student, requires a healthy dose of common sense. The simplest rule of thumb might be to use formally prepared Project ILPs only when the "P" in "ILP" clearly is called for. That is, if a formal "Plan" is needed in order for production and learning to be efficient, then one should be written. If, on the other hand, the major project tasks or any sub-parts thereof can be accomplished as readily in a less formal fashion, then such "writing down" of task steps, alternative actions, learning resources, etc., should not be required.

A second guideline is that formally written Project ILPs should be used whenever the teacher wants to focus student attention on the *processes* as well as the content of learning. Mastery of the processes of issue resolving and "product" making frequently is a more important learning outcome than is content familiarity or mastery. Such processes are the foundation for life-long independent productivity and related learning and, as such, they are very important tools in a rapidly changing world.

The third guideline relates to both teacher and student accountability and evaluation. The teacher should develop or require written Project ILPs whenever (1) the written ILP will contribute to student self-accountability and self-evaluation, or (2) the written ILP will facilitate teacher accountability for and evaluation of student learning. One practical way in which the written ILP may contribute to accountability is when it is used as a "contract" between the teacher and the student. A second way is when the written ILP is evaluated in its completed form by the teacher and the student. The written ILP, as an artifact of how the student approached the project and what was learned, contains a wealth of data to document the nature and amount of student learning that occurred.

## References
*(USE section)*

Burton, W.H. *The Nature and Direction of Learning.* New York: D. Appleton and Company, 1929, pp. 254-276.

Charters, W.W. The Limitations of the Project. *Addresses and Proceedings of the Fifty-ninth Annual Meeting of the National Education Association*, 1921, *59*, 428-430.

Kilpatrick, W.H. The Project Method. *Teachers College Record*, September 1918, *19*, 319-335.

Kilpatrick, W.H. Dangers and Difficulties of the Project Method and How to Overcome Them—A Symposium. *Teachers College Record*, September 1921, *22*, 283-321.

Kilpatrick, W.H. *Foundations of Method: Informal Talks on Teaching.* New York: The Macmillan Company, 1925, pp. 344-371.

Tolman, K.G. and P.G. Kapfer. Transactional Areas of Medicine. Unpublished curriculum development design, 1976.

Woodruff, A.D. *The Life-Involvement Model of Education (LIM): A System Description.* Salt Lake City, Utah: Bureau of Educational Research, University of Utah, 1973, p. 68.

# II.

# OPERATIONAL DESCRIPTION

This section will provide a broad overview of the two Project ILP instructional designs—the Issue Project ILP for issue resolution or goal choosing, and the Production Project ILP for "production" activities or goal achievement. Prior to looking at operational aspects of the Project ILP designs, however, several possible principles of learning will be examined for their relevance to designing instruction in general and for their impact on Issue and Production Projects in particular.

## Principles of Learning for
## Designing Instruction

There are a number of well-documented basic assumptions about human behavior upon which we can depend. According to Woodruff (1973), three of the most important of these are the following:

(1) People learn what they practice.

(2) Change in behavior is to a large extent a function of the consequences of the behavior.

(3) The impact of any given learning experience on the learner's out-of-school life is directly proportional to the reality and authenticity of the learning experience.

*15*

If examined carefully, these assumptions have direct and pervasive implications for teaching/learning designs at all levels.

*Principle No. 1: People learn what they practice.* This principle should be understood in its literal sense. The learner does not learn what he does not practice. Whatever the learner *does* within a given instructional setting is typically what he will *learn* to do, whether it is to listen to the teacher, to take notes, to follow directions, to practice procedures, to use rational processes, or to engage directly in some creative or utilitarian production activity. To activate this principle, every ability to be learned must be literally practiced, and it must be practiced enough times to produce mastery. In addition, the ability must be practiced at successively higher levels of complexity until it reaches the desired level.

For example, the piano student studies "theory" in direct association with learning to play sharps, flats, chords, and the like. This is both *learning while doing* in the case of theory and *learning by doing* in the case of piano playing. The history student learns to differentiate between primary and secondary historical sources while collecting data for a brief historical study. Similarly, the surgery resident "really learns" abdominal anatomy the night before performing his or her first appendectomy. In all of these examples, the learning was focused by the student's knowledge of how that learning was going to be used *right away*. Thus, the student not only learned some content, but he or she also decided *what* to learn. The consequences of learning the wrong things, or of not learning the right things well enough, would become readily apparent to the student in these "on the job" behaviors.

This principle of learning has clear implications for the design of Project ILPs. Because people appear to learn what and only what they practice, these life-based instructional designs emphasize the basic processes that are engaged in, in one form or another, by virtually all people throughout their lives. These are (1) choosing one's own goals (issue resolving), (2) materializing one's own goals ("product" making), and (3) learning while doing these two. Thus, in every Project ILP the student is practicing (and hopefully learning) a basic essential life-based skill. If we wish students to be effective as in-life planners and decision-makers, then our classrooms must be filled with exciting planning and decision-making activities rather than with often passive "school behaviors."

*Principle No. 2: Change in behavior is to a large extent a function of the consequences of the behavior.* Without ignoring possible genetic elements in behavior, this principle emphasizes the fact that in significant learning, as in life, the learner must go through a complete cycle of behavior. This cycle consists of perceiving a situation, deciding how to act upon it, acting out one's decision, recognizing the consequences that result from the decision, and redirecting one's actions in the light of those consequences.

This cycle of behavior can be activated only if the student is allowed to practice the abilities that he is to learn. To use an analogy, learning must be organized so that the student rather than the teacher is the primary "actor" in the theater of learning, with the teacher at the edge of the stage in the role of coach, mentor, monitor, and facilitator. Implementation of this cycle requires that the student be provided with opportunities to *engage directly with the phenomena* that are involved in each ability that he must learn. (This is one reason that the idea of using phenomena as a way of defining content for Project ILPs was advanced earlier in this book.) The student then must be allowed to experience directly, without undue intervention from the teacher, the consequences of his learning actions, activities, and choices.

*Principle No. 3: The impact of any given learning*

*experience on the learner's out-of-school life is directly proportional to the reality and authenticity of the learning experience.* This very important principle may be used to guide the effective operation of programs in which Issue and Production Project ILPs are used. This principle incorporates the following three interesting facts that continually surface to threaten educational programs that do not employ life-based approaches (Woodruff, 1973):

(1)   The degree of transfer of a learned ability from a school setting to a life setting is proportional to the degree of identity between practice conditions and usage conditions.

(2)   Commitment on the learner's part is proportional to his or her own perceived personal value of what is to be learned or done.

(3)   The learner's effort is usually proportional to his or her commitment to the learning tasks.

To activate this principle fully, the student must act upon the same phenomena in the same way and under the same conditions in school as he will in life, including on the job. Furthermore, the knowledge, understandings, and skills typically taught in school must be made subservient to and learned in direct association with their usage in making and executing the same kinds of decisions as are made in life. Therefore, schools must be life-like settings in which the student's commitment to learning grows naturally out of the value which he perceives that learning to have for himself personally.

Although other reliable facts about how people learn could be discussed here, the several we have just looked at are sufficient to provide sound direction for an operational description of the two Project ILPs. The remainder of this section, therefore, contains an introductory overview of how the two Project ILP instructional designs work.

## Issue Project ILP

The Issue Project ILP is designed to provide students with opportunities to practice the possible steps involved in resolving issues in systematic and rational ways. The use of the Issue Project ILP is based on the assumption that consistent application of systematic procedures to the resolution of issues should produce *more rational* decisions.*

Picture yourself in a classroom with a new group of elementary, secondary, or even college-level students. The chances are fairly certain that these students have seldom if ever applied systematic procedures to the resolution of an issue. (They have resolved plenty of issues, to be sure, and they may have done so more or less rationally, but the key idea here centers on the use of *systematic procedures*.) The students may not know even how to state an issue, or that an "issue" (What should be done about ... ?) is different from a "problem" (What is the "right answer" to ... ?). As a teacher, where does one start?

From what we know about learning, the most productive course of action might be to ignore definitions for the moment and begin instead with a concrete experience. To do so, one could first prepare a list of value-laden phenomena. For example, the following list might be useful at several academic levels:

(1) Alcoholism
(2) Abortion
(3) Drug abuse
(4) Taxes
(5) Unemployment
(6) Petroleum consumption

*It should be noted that such rationally-based decisions may or may not be *better* decisions. This is a determination that would depend, of course, on the components of each individual's basic values structure.

   (7)  Nuclear waste
   (8)  Pornography
   (9)  White collar crime
(10)  Etc.

The second step in introducing students to Issue Project ILPs might be to choose one of these phenomena for in-depth study by all students in the class, following which the entire class could share what they had learned. As a structure for the sharing, the teacher—acting as recorder—could translate the selected phenomenon into an issue—"What should be done about ... ?" Student discussion of values related to the issue, of alternative goals that would resolve the issue, and of the probable consequences of carrying out each of those goals could be recorded by the teacher. Although an individual student might not have explored all of the issue-related possibilities regarding the selected phenomenon, especially during an initial experience of this sort, the collective inquiry of an entire class might be rather complete at this point. One or more such group experiences with issue resolution could set the stage for independent student use of Issue Project ILPs, particularly as students become attuned to sorting out issues that are individually meaningful.

*Improving issue resolution.* Most teachers at the elementary school level would agree that accomplishing what has just been described may require a good deal of time, patient teaching, and practice. However, the occasion will come sooner or later (sooner for secondary and college students) when the fundamental issue resolving process just outlined becomes so familiar as to be "old hat." *Before* that time arrives, the teacher should introduce strategies for improving each step of the issue resolution process.

For example, we mentioned earlier that issues and problems are not the same. As these terms are being used here, an issue involves value choices; a problem does not. An electrical outlet that does not work is an issue only so long as no one has decided (1) to fix it, and (2) when to fix it. Cost and time values are involved in resolving these simple issues. However, once the goal has been set, for example, to fix the outlet next Saturday morning, the issues have been resolved. The malfunctioning outlet has been reduced to the level of a problem or two. For example, "Why doesn't it work?" and "Should it be fixed or replaced?" These are essentially operational decisions rather than goal-choosing decisions. Understanding this difference contributes to increased student ability to define issues.

Each of the basic steps in issue resolution lends itself to similar improvement. For example, extensive work has been done on the teaching of values analysis. In addition, methods have been developed for teaching students ways of judging the qualifications of "authorities" representing all sides of a given issue. The details of these and other sophisticated methods for improving issue resolution are beyond the scope of this book. Even so, use of Issue Project ILPs, when combined with the basic supporting behaviors that will be demonstrated later, may make a qualitative difference in students' lives, both inside and outside of school.

**Production Project ILP**

Teachers have been involving students in "product" making for many years. Christmas programs, science fairs, woodworking projects, bake sales, newspapers, and radio stations are a few of many examples that can be seen in schools. In some classes, such projects are as much a part of the on-going subject matter as the more traditional conceptual and verbal content. In other classes and for other teachers, projects are a one-time or a sometime thing. In a few situations, projects are non-existent. In our view, "product" making projects should be an integral part of every course at every level. In addition, such projects should be carefully planned so that conceptual learning is integrated with its functional use.

The "product" making goals of every profession, trade, and service are prime sources for Production Project goals. The choice of a goal for a Production Project ILP may result from formal issue resolution processes or simply from an informal decision. Any number of possibilities exist between these two, of course. The point is that the student chooses a *personal* goal, something that *he or she wants* to procure or produce.

One way of introducing students to Production Project ILPs is to select a "product" that (1) has wide student appeal, and (2) is simple enough that students can perform all of the production steps at the outset. The reason for the first criterion is motivation. The purpose of the second criterion is to isolate, in the students' first experience with a formal Production Project ILP, the teaching of production processes from other types of learning. Such simplification has obvious teaching advantages. But it also has certain risks. For example, simple procedure following, without concomitant conceptual learning, can become a comfortable and rewarding mode of operation, whereas the basic idea behind Production Project ILPs is that the procedures involved will "carry" significant new learning. As a result, when the teacher determines that the students are ready to add content learning to the practice of production processes, careful groundwork may be necessary in order to get students "on task." The Production Project ILP provides a structure through which operational choices may be made for solving these and other teaching problems.

*Improving "product" making.* Students must learn how to choose and properly delimit goals for Production Project

ILPs. This is true of the youngster who may "bite off more (or less) than he can chew." The same may be said for the graduate student selecting a thesis topic or the medical student selecting a patient problem for computer-simulated diagnosis and management. In all of these cases, the content index idea discussed in the USE section of this book is a helpful guide and idea stimulator for student selection of "product" goals.

In addition, once the potential "products" in a subject area have been identified, a pivotal instructional decision involves the promotion of dependency behaviors versus independency behaviors in students. Should the potential "products" be doled out one at a time by the teacher, or should the possibilities be exposed all at once to students? Or, something in between? In what form should the potential "products" be exposed? How should the teacher be involved in the choices that students make? The answers to these questions depend on many factors that are situation specific. There is no "right" answer for all times, teachers, programs, and students. The only requirement is that the teacher be aware of and attempt to answer such questions according to his or her own circumstances.

Choosing a goal is only the first basic step. Clarifying and defining the goal by listing specifications for what it should "look like" when it is achieved also is an important skill. In addition, the student must learn that a task analysis, however simple or complex, is required in order to identify production steps, and that the objects and procedures involved in those steps are the subject matter content that must be learned. The understanding and use by students of these processes will improve their production efforts.

Other items may be considered as well. Of particular importance are actions that contribute to focused learning about the designated subject matter content. Some of these will be discussed later in this book. The critical idea at this point is that all such "product" making procedures are *life-based processes* that have been synthesized for school use.

**Reference**
*(OPERATIONAL DESCRIPTION section)*

Woodruff, A.D. Designing a Curriculum for Humanistic Behavior. Paper presented at the National Art Education Association Conference, San Diego, California, April, 1973.

# III.

# DESIGN FORMAT

Formats and examples of the two Project ILP designs are presented in this section.* The Issue Project ILP was named to reflect its emphasis on the processes used to resolve issues. The outcomes of such projects are rationally selected goals. The name of the second ILP design, the Production Project ILP, also captures the processes that are involved. The Production Project ILP leads to outcomes that include any kind of material or non-material "product" that a person may make, buy, build, construct, create, invent, or the like. Both of these Project ILP instructional designs also may include selected inquiry processes. These inquiry processes are discussed as appropriate in the following paragraphs. The basic components of the two Project ILP designs are shown in outline form in Figure 3.

**Issue Project ILP**
Good teachers have always focused student attention on

*The basic processes that are carried by the two Project ILP designs are discussed in detail in this section of the book. The explication of these processes relies heavily on a number of in-house documents of the Life Involvement Model (LIM) Project (Kapfer, 1973; Kapfer and Kapfer, 1975; Woodruff, 1973; and Woodruff, 1974). Because these materials were adapted for use throughout this section, they are cited *in toto* here rather than at each point of use or influence.

*Figure 3*

*Project ILP Format Outlines*

---

**Issue Project ILP: Format Outline**

---

1.  *Issue* (What should be done about . . .?)

2.  *Values* (Why are you concerned?)

3.  *Alternative Actions*

4.  *Where You Could Learn About Each Action*

5.  *Possible Results of Each Action*

6.  *Your Choice (Goal)*

7.  *Reasons*

---

**Production Project ILP: Format Outline**

---

1.  *"Product" (Goal)*

2.  *Specifications*

3.  *Steps You Will Follow*

4.  *Where You Could Learn About Each Step*

5.  *Objects and/or Procedures Involved in Doing Each Step*

6.  *Test*

potential issues inherent in the phenomena being studied. The use of Issue Project ILPs insures the systematic consideration and resolution of such issues. As indicated in Figure 3, Issue Project ILPs contain the following seven parts: (1) the name of the object or event that is the central focus of the issue, (2) a list of the values (of oneself, of important others, and of society) that will be affected one way or another by the issue's resolution, (3) alternative actions for resolving the issue, (4) learning resources that could be employed for learning about each alternative action, (5) the possible results that one could anticipate from the selection of each alternative action, (6) the alternative or combination of alternatives selected for resolving the issue, and (7) the rationale for selecting a particular alternative action. The names of these seven parts may be used as headings for organizing teacher or student responses while planning or carrying out an issue resolving episode. Each of the seven parts of the Issue Project ILP format is described in the following seven sub-sections. A complete example of the Issue Project instructional design, employing a single issue, is provided in the final sub-section.

*Statement of the issue.* Issue resolution in life is a response to an unsatisfactory condition for which a change is desired. Therefore, in life-based programs, the issue resolution process is designed to result in the selection of a goal that will accomplish the desired change. In some instances, goal selection is quite simple and does not require a formal process. In many other cases, the choice of a goal is complex and its impact on one's values is important enough to the individual or the group to warrant the use of systematic issue resolution processes.

As noted previously, issues typically are stated in the form, "What should be done about . . . ?" Filling in the ellipsis in the preceding sentence with the name of the object or event that is involved amounts to identifying an unsatisfactory condition or issue.

In learning to state issues accurately and concisely, it is essential to clearly distinguish issues from problems. As we are using these terms, issues differ from problems in three significant ways. First, problems have "right" answers that are identifiable on the basis of natural laws. In contrast, an issue does not have a single "right" answer because the resolution of an issue is dependent upon the values of the concerned individual or group. Individuals and groups of individuals have a variety of value patterns and, therefore, different "right" answers. Second, problems may be stated in a form that allows a "yes" or "no" response. An issue, on the other hand, is stated in a form that clearly requires the identification of alternative resolutions. Third, and most important, problems do not *directly* involve human values. Issues do. The reason for this last distinction is that, strictly speaking, a problem does not exist until after a person has chosen a goal or, in other words, until after he has already resolved an issue.

Issues may be classified for our purposes into two major categories—group issues and personal issues. Issues that lend themselves to group resolution might include the following:

What should be done about . . .
    (1) The library security system?
    (2) Salary and benefits?
    (3) Recession?
    (4) The national debt?
    (5) The balance of payments?
    (6) Political campaign financing?
    (7) Right to die?
    (8) Amnesty?
    (9) Victimless crimes?
    (10) Vandalism?
    (11) Welfare?
    (12) Etc.

Examples of personal issues are as follows:

> What should be done about . . .
>   (1) My appearance?
>   (2) My physical condition?
>   (3) My social relations?
>   (4) My self-image and feelings of competence?
>   (5) My earning power?
>   (6) Etc.

The phenomena named in these two sets of examples may be "rationed" one at a time to students or they may be included in a content index prepared for student use. The latter approach has the distinct advantage of creating more favorable conditions for the development of student self-initiative and independence in learning. The exact form that such an index could take would depend on the subject matter involved and on the maturity level of the student. In addition, the student must be sufficiently in tune with reality to respond to issues when he or she sees them. That is, phenomena that are unknown to a student or that are known only from one point of view are not likely to be perceived by the student as the focus of meaningful and relevant issues. For this reason, we would expect most issues to grow out of the student's personal experiences with phenomena.

For example, a student's personal experience related to viewing television advertising could lead to the issue, "What should be done about the type of TV advertising that promotes goods or services that are not in the public's best interest?" The average student's sensitivity, prior to studying such advertising, may range from a total lack of knowledge to a vague awareness both of governmental controls and of industry-imposed advertising codes. Students must learn how to relate to such issues and how to deal with them rationally.

*Identification of the values involved.* A useful way of

identifying the values involved in an issue is to ask oneself the question, "What am I trying to gain or to protect for myself and for others in the resolution of this issue?" This question can be asked either by an individual or a group. When the question is asked by a group, processes of compromise or consensus must be used in identifying the group's values. Subsequent individual commitment to whatever option is chosen by the group for resolving the issue is dependent upon the degree of match between an individual's personal values and the group values that have been decided upon. Recognition of this fact goes a long way toward explaining why issue resolution by a group does not always result in *total* group effort toward achieving the selected goal. In addition, resolution of one issue frequently has an impact on the resolution of related issues. Therefore it is not always possible for an individual or a group to consider only one issue at a time.

For example, the issue "What should be done about inflation?" is closely related to one's interests and values concerning (1) preserving the buying power of people living on fixed incomes, (2) maintaining an easy money supply for long-term borrowing for home mortgages, (3) attaining an unemployment level of less than three percent of the work force, and the like. In completing this step of an Issue Project ILP on inflation, the student should demonstrate that he recognizes the varying impact of inflation on his own and others' values. In addition, he should perceive that the resolution of the inflation issue is closely related to issues such as the following:

    What should be done about . . .
        (1)    Wage and price controls?
        (2)    Worldwide monetary stability?
        (3)    Foreign trade?
        (4)    Federal spending?
        (5)    Etc.

At a more personal level, the issue "What should be done about my health?" involves values such as the following: (1) I want to feel good, (2) I want to look good, (3) I want to have the necessary stamina for participating in individual and group sports, (4) I want to live a long and healthy life, and (5) I want to enhance my mental productivity. Again, the student should demonstrate that he or she has thoughtfully identified the issue-related values that are involved.

The values that have been identified and characterized according to their impact on oneself and others now are ready to be prioritized. The student is responsible for identifying those values that he or she wishes to maximize and those that he or she should minimize. Some values are more important to us in certain circumstances than are others. This is not to say that we need to be wishy-washy about our values. Rather, we must recognize that there are positives and negatives for alternatives that we might select in the resolution of almost any issue. For example, most of us value honesty and yet we will say to a friend we have not seen for 15 years, "You are the same old Jim!" even though half of his hair is gone and he has put on 40 pounds. Obviously, in such a situation, we value the friend's feelings more than we value unvarnished honesty.

Both the identification of one's values related to an issue and the ranking of those values are greatly influenced by one's depth of understanding of the issue. For this reason, the values section of an Issue Project ILP should be shaped *by the student* as he or she identifies or studies possible alternative actions for resolving the issue and as he or she increasingly understands the possible results of each action. It is the teacher's responsibility to look for evidence that the student has returned to the values section of the Issue Project ILP and has expanded, revised, and/or reordered his or her values while engaged in the Project.

For example, some of the initial student-identified values involved in the issue "What should be done about snowball throwing on the playground?" might be as follows: (1) I want to have fun on the playground, (2) I don't want anyone to get hurt, (3) I don't want to be "ganged up" on, and (4) I want to abide by the established playground rules, whatever they are. These four values may be ranked 24 different ways (4 x 3 x 2 x 1). Because of the potential for serious eye injury resulting from snowball throwing, school administrators often are sorely tempted to establish hard-and-fast rules concerning this type of activity. However, the classroom Issue Project ILP, in which students identify and rank the values that are involved, might prove to be a much more effective way of obtaining student commitment to whatever alternatives are chosen than would be the issuing of rules and the subsequent necessity of "police action" for their enforcement. Students who study this issue might call upon a local general practitioner or ophthalmologist to learn about specific examples of eye injuries resulting from snowball throwing. In the course of collecting information, the students might learn that many of the eye injuries resulted from children throwing warm "old" snow that had turned into iceballs when compacted. In addition, they might learn that the large majority of children who received injuries were not actually engaged in snowball throwing themselves but rather were caught unaware by stray snowballs. As a result of such learning, the students might decide to add the following new values to their list, probably reordering some items in the process: (1) children should have the right to organize snowball fights under optimal snow conditions, and (2) children not involved in snowball throwing should have the right to play on the playground without danger of being hit by snowballs.

*Identification of alternative actions.* Generating alternative solutions for an issue can be a very creative process, sometimes requiring only the imaginative use of the current knowledge of a group of students. An example of such a process occurred in a sixth grade class which had assumed a Sub-for-Santa project. Because of school district financial problems, buses were not available for field trips, and thus the students as a total group could not deliver their Chirstmas gifts to the Sub-for-Santa family. The teacher, rather than telling the class that she and several class members could deliver the packages in her private car, presented the class with the issue, "What should be done about delivering the gifts to the Sub-for-Santa family?" In this case, the students had at the outset all of the facts they needed for resolving the issue and, therefore, they could focus on identifying their values, alternative resolutions, and probable consequences. They identified a large number of inventive alternatives, including the one that the teacher privately favored. And, of most importance, they were satisfied with their choice (which, as it turned out, was the same as the teacher's).

Alternatives are not so readily identified for many issues, and in order to avoid triviality in such cases the student must engage in focused study. The teacher should monitor regularly the adequacy of such student work. Many people, when attempting to resolve a difficult issue, locate authorities who have spoken or written about the issue. In so doing, people hope to identify viable alternatives from which to choose, based on their own particular sets of values. The sources of authority may be found in various print and non-print library materials as well as among respected peers, colleagues, relatives, clergymen, and so forth.

To review a point made earlier, it should be recognized that the processes being discussed here, although basic and important, do not represent the totality of what the student can learn concerning the generation of alternative actions.

Rather, the processes that have been described thus far may be thought of as the basic behaviors that must be on-going before additional ideas and strategies may be added.

*Where you could learn about each action.* The same sources that are used for identifying alternatives also may be used for investigating them. The purpose of this section of the Issue Project ILP format is to encourage the student to list inquiry sources in an orderly and complete fashion. Depending on the age of the student and other considerations, the teacher may require a complete bibliographic citation for each source that is used.

*Possible results of each action.* The investigation of each alternative includes four basic areas of concern. First, the student is attempting to anticipate in rather broad terms what is involved in carrying out each alternative. He is not yet attempting to conduct a thorough task anslysis for each alternative. A task analysis is often a time consuming process that goes well beyond the level of understanding that typically is necessary for the purpose of choosing an alternative. Second, the student is trying to anticipate the consequences of each alternative for himself and for others. Such consequences usually are described in one form or another by the authorities that are studied. Third, the student is attempting to identify the beliefs that are basic to each of the alternatives so that he or she is in a better position to examine inconsistencies in his or her own beliefs and to settle them either by changing those beliefs or by learning to accept the inconsistencies that may exist. Fourth, the student is attempting to observe how others whom he or she respects have weighed the alternatives in terms of the net effect of the alternatives on their own values and on the values they ascribe to others. This allows the student to more rationally judge the alternatives for their potential effect on his or her *own* values.

The student should treat the beliefs and values of other people as *facts* about those people that should be taken into consideration in determining his or her position regarding an issue. Even admonitions that the student may have received regarding the issue should be viewed at this point as *facts* about how the admonisher believes the student should act *rather than as advice* that the student must follow. The essential question that the student should ask of himself is how he can obtain the *most* of what he is attempting to gain or to protect *for himself and for others.*

The possible consequences of each alternative include both the *end state* of the action and whatever is involved in *carrying out* the action. In other words, both the means and the ends that are involved in any alternative resolution of an issue have an impact on the student's values and, therefore, both should be taken into account when studying the alternatives. The teacher should monitor both of these factors when checking this section of the student's Issue Project ILP. An example can be seen in the issue of controlling inflation. Two alternatives, namely wage-price controls and reduced government spending, may be equally capable of influencing inflationary trends in a downward direction. However, wage-price controls could necessitate creating a new bureaucracy for their administration, whereas mechanisms may already exist for administering the consequences of decreased government spending. This difference in implementation probably will have an impact on the range of values that may be identified concerning the issue.

*Your choice (goal).* The alternative action chosen by the student should be identified in the appropriate space on the Issue Project ILP format. By actually recording a choice or goal, the student assumes an assertive outlook rather than a "whatever will be, will be" mentality. Also, by making conscious choices, the student is learning that he has a certain amount of control over his environment. The student's identification of a goal would conclude his work on the Issue Project ILP if it were not for the fact that most people are responsible to someone for their decisions, whether that "someone" is a teacher, parent, spouse, employer, employee, peer, or, in the last analysis, themselves. This factor of student responsibility for the value-based choices that he or she makes is carried out by systematically "justifying" those choices, a process which is discussed in greater detail in the next section.

*Reasons for the choice.* "Justifying" one's choice does not mean proving that it is right or wrong. Rather, the student should be able to describe how the particular alternative selected affects the values that he or she is trying to preserve or to gain for himself and others. When discussing this particular step with a student, the teacher's responsibility is to make sure that the student has, in fact, considered all of the alternatives, that he or she has considered the steps involved in carrying out each alternative, and that he or she is aware of the probable consequences of each alternative. If the teacher's personal choice of an alternative should happen to differ from that of the student, it is quite in order for the teacher to inform the student of this difference and to justify it. In so doing, the teacher is modeling for the student how one justifies by reference to one's values the choice of an alternative resolution to an issue. The student, of course, is under no obligation to accept for himself the teacher's choice or values. Rather, the student should consider the teacher's choice and the justification of it simply as additional facts related to the issue.

For example, let us assume that an academically talented student is completing an Issue Project ILP in which alternative careers are being studied. He probably could make virtually any career choice and justify it adequately on the basis of his own values. Whatever his choice, the teacher is responsible for making sure that the student is aware of the consequences of his career choice as well as the potential outcomes of other possible choices. If this highly gifted student chooses a career for which a high school diploma is the only requirement, the teacher also may wish to discuss with him the extent to which the student's knowledge of his talent was taken into account in his resolution of the career-choice issue.

*An example of an Issue Project ILP.* A wealth and variety of examples are important to accurate concept formation, particularly when dealing with somewhat involved concepts. We have attempted in the preceding discussion of the Issue Project ILP to include just such a rich variety of examples. However, the question still may remain, "What does an Issue Project ILP look like?" Figure 4 is designed as a response to this need.

The issue in the Project ILP in Figure 4 is, "What should be done about legal or illegal drug abuse when I am personally faced with drug-related situations?" This issue is as current today as it was ten or 100 years ago. The details may mutate with the times, but the basic issue of personal drug use does not. It is an issue that most people face initially sometime between the ages of ten and twenty, and periodically thereafter. (We all have heard of instances of heavy drug use during the first decade of life, but hopefully these are the exceptions rather than the rule.) The particular Issue Project ILP provided in Figure 4 is designed for "middle school" students—perhaps from ages ten to early teens. In any case, in this example we are assuming a degree of naiveté that is characteristic of children who may have taken various medicines for childhood illnesses and who have seen people using tobacco and alcohol, but who are essentially unfamiliar with broader concepts regarding drugs and drug use.

*Figure 4*

*Issue Project ILP on Drug Abuse*


**Issue Project ILP**

*Issue*:      What should be done about legal or illegal drug abuse when
             I am personally faced with drug-related situations? (For use
             by middle school students who are essentially unfamiliar
             with drug abuse.)


*Values*:    (Why am I ...................... concerned?)
                            student's name

             Listed below are some ideas that may or may not say what
             you think. Change them, accept them, and/or add to them
             as you study and talk to people whom you respect.

             (1)    I want to face the problem of illegal drug use rather
                    than being uninformed about it.

             (2)    I want to make up my own mind about using
                    different kinds of drugs.

             (3)    I want to anticipate drug-related situations so that I
                    am better able to handle them if and when they
                    occur. In other words, I want to think ahead about
                    what I will do if I find myself with friends who want
                    me to try one drug or another.

             (4)    I want to be helped by prescription and "over-the-
                    counter" drugs. I want to know when I should and
                    should not use them.

             (5)    I do not want to hurt my mind or my body by the
                    wrong use of drugs.


*(Continued)*

*Figure 4 (Continued)*

(6) I do not want to hurt someone else by the way I use drugs.

(7) I do not want to "rat" on my friends.

(8) Etc.

*Alternative Actions*:

Following are some quick and easy options of the kind that you might think of at first. Study them, using the ideas in the next section, and then make up your own list. Your list should contain potential actions that are less "obvious" or superficial.

(1) Do not use any drugs.

(2) Do not use any illegal drugs.

(3) Do exactly what my parents tell me to.

(4) Go along with what my friends are doing.

(5) Try anything once.

\* \* \* \* \* \* \* \* \* \* \* \* \* \* \*

Write your list here or on the reverse side.

*Where You Could Learn About Each Action*:

There are numerous films, filmstrips, audio tapes, books, pamphlets, worksheets, and self-tests on drugs and drug abuse. Words that will help you find media are . . .

*(Continued)*

*Figure 4 (Continued)*

DRUGS
ALCOHOL
NARCOTICS
TOBACCO

Talk to people. Get their ideas about drug related . . .

VALUES
ALTERNATIVES
RESULTS

*Possible Results of Each Action*:

As you study the issue, try to sort out fact from fiction and data from beliefs. Remember that the "results" of an action may affect one's body, mind, feelings about self and others, religious beliefs, future, etc. List here or on the reverse side the possible results of each action.

*Your Choice (Goal)*:   .............................................................................

*Reasons*:   What *values* do you really care about and how does your choice affect them?

**Production Project ILP**

As was indicated earlier in Figure 3, Production Project ILPs contain the following six parts: (1) a word or phrase that clearly identifies the "product" (goal) that the student wishes to produce or achieve, (2) a list of the specifications that the "product" must meet in order to satisfy the student's goal, (3) a task analysis containing the steps that must be followed in order to produce the "product" or achieve the goal, (4) a list of learning resources (human resources, realia, and media) that contain the subject matter involved in achieving the "product" or goal, (5) a list of phenomena (objects and/or procedures) with which the student must be competent in order to carry out each task step, and (6) a final test of some sort that permits evaluation, first, of the "product" as measured against its specifications and, second, of the student's conceptual learning and ability to communicate about that learning.

The "format sheet" for the Production Project ILP consists of a convenient arrangement on paper of six brief headings that correspond to these six parts (such as the headings presented in Figure 3). The particular vocabulary and arrangement of headings on the format sheet will depend largely on the maturity of the students who will use it. An additional determining factor might be whether the Production Project is planned primarily by the teacher or by the student.

In the following pages, each of the six parts of the Production Project ILP will be discussed in detail. A single "product" will be used for illustrative purposes throughout this discussion—the goal of constructing a terrarium. This topic was selected because it is dealt with in one form or another at almost all levels in school textbooks and other media. The most likely subject areas in which this topic might be found include gardening, nature, the environment, science, ecology, interior decorating, horticulture, botany, soil chemistry, microbiology, and so forth. A complete teacher-constructed secondary school Production Project ILP on building a terrarium will conclude this section.

*Identification of the "product" (goal).* The "product" of a Production Project ILP should have a definite form. It should have a set of characteristics or specifications by which it can be recognized when it exists. The Production Project ILP is not an indefinite line of development or activity, nor is it a repeating cyclical behavior. The name of the Production Project and the name of the "product" typically are the same. Obviously, the "product" should be named as accurately as possible.

As pointed out earlier, "products" may be made, developed, bought, sold, grown, invented, composed, arranged, and the like. A "product" may take any one of several forms, of which the following are examples: a tangible article, a personal attribute, a composition, a developed idea (as in art, music, research, etc.), a staged event, and a plan for action. Both the teacher and the student are responsible for determining that the goal chosen by the student for a Production Project ILP is really a "product" and that it is educationally worthwhile for the particular student.

*Specifications.* Sufficient time and effort should be expended by both the student and the teacher on the development of specifications for the "product" of a Production Project ILP. The specifications determine whether the "product" will be mundane or whether it will have elements of creativity within it. In addition, the specifications may be written such that they require no new learning by the student or such that the student is required to carry out task steps that do require the gaining of new skills and understandings. Although there may be rare exceptions, in general the production tasks should require the development of new competencies that are widely useful in life, that are best learned in formal school settings, and that involve adjunctive behaviors such as reading, communicating, and calculating. Even so, the student must be capable of *approaching* the project with his or her existing competencies. That is, the student should be sufficiently knowledgeable about the "product" to be able to plan for its production in an intelligent manner so that the probability of success is maximized. In addition, the "product" as specified must be achieveable within the time the student can be expected to remain motivated.

As indicated above, we are using the example of a terrarium to illustrate the use of the Production Project ILP format. Subsequent to listing "terrarium" as the goal of the Production Project ILP, the student should be able to list initial criteria such as the following: (1) the terrarium container should be 18 to 24 inches high and 12 to 18 inches in diameter, (2) the soil planting surface should be sloped in order to better display plants at different heights, and (3) plants should be utilized that are compatible with one another and that do not require more space than the jar size will accommodate.

Each of the sections of the Production Project ILP should be examined carefully by the teacher as it is being developed by the student. For example, following the student's initial listing of specifications for the terrarium, it may be apparent to the teacher that the student needs to engage in exploratory study in order to add other specifications. That is, the teacher may be aware that even a cursory examination of terrariums in florist, grocery, or discount stores would reveal information of the following types: (1) plants may be selected to display a variety of shades of green ranging from pale yellow-green to near-black tones, (2) plants also may be chosen for the purpose of introducing several leaf textures ranging from glossy and silk-like to furry and variegated, (3) small figures may be added to create a primary focus of visual interest, and (4) colored stones may be used to form a center path that will carry the eye further into the scene.

The unique roles of the teacher and student in using ILPs are illustrated in the preceding paragraph. The teacher's primary responsibility at this point is to make sure that the student does in fact gain new knowledge, understanding, and competence from engaging in a Production Project ILP. At the same time, the student is responsible for responding with personal commitment to the opportunities for such learning that are embedded in the "product" that he or she is producing.

Exploratory study, just illustrated, may give way to highly focused study during the course of the production activity. For example, while searching for specifications, the student may notice that specialized planting media may be purchased for terrariums. Thus, the student may add a specification concerning the number and types of layers of planting media that he or she will use, including potting soil, charcoal, sand or gravel, and moss. This specification may be dependent on the nature of the jar that the student selected (whether it is narrow-necked, wide-topped, aquarium-type, or domed) and on the kinds of plants that he or she selected (tropical, semi-tropical, or desert). This specification also may be dependent on other factors perhaps totally unknown to the student unless he engages in considerable focused inquiry on plant nutrition in closed environments.

In summary, when examining the student's Production Project specifications, the teacher may be concerned with questions such as the following: (1) Do the specifications display creativity? (2) Are they written at an expectation level that is appropriate for the ability of the student? (3) Will the student be required to gain new competencies in order to meet the specifications?

*Steps you will follow.* One of the properties that is essential for a Production Project ILP to be educationally useful is that the task must be sufficiently complex to require planning for effective accomplishment. Task planning requires careful analysis of what is involved in producing the "product" such that its specifications are met. Because the student either must *be* competent or must be able to *become* competent in performing the task steps, the teacher should be concerned that these steps are stated at a level of inclusiveness that the student can handle at his stage of development. This may be illustrated by comparing two possible sets of task steps. For example, the task steps for the terrarium project might be listed as follows: (1) prepare for making a terrarium, (2) construct the terrarium, and (3) add finishing touches to the terrarium. Or, the task steps, at least the initial ones, might be structured in this way: (1) obtain the terrarium container, and (2) on the basis of the size and shape of the container, make a list of the plants and other materials that will be purchased or collected. It is evident that the steps in the first set are so inclusive as to be almost useless to the novice terrarium builder. The second set, by contrast, actually represent an expansion of "Prepare for making a terrarium," and are written at a more useful level of inclusiveness.

As implied above, the materials that are needed for carrying out the Production Project also are a part of the task analysis. These may fall into two categories. First, raw materials or "means" must be chosen, located, secured, prepared for processing, and processed into the "product." Second, specialized tools or equipment may be needed to accomplish particular steps in the project. Both of these types of materials should be listed by the student as a part of the task steps for which they are needed. For example, if one of the task steps in the terrarium project is to "Place the plants in the terrarium soil mixture," then the basic materials needed might include (1) the terrarium container with the soil in place, (2) the plants, and (3) planting tools such as a funnel, a shovel, wooden dowel sticks, a plant "placer," and a tamper.

*Where you could learn about each step.* The student should record citations to the resources that are used. Both consultant sources and library resources might be listed. Two purposes may be identified for this activity. First, an analysis of each production step should be carried out so that the *phenomena* are identified upon which the student must "act" competently. Second, the *properties* of the phenomena that are critical for mastering the competence (that is, for performing each task step) should be identified.

For example, "planting" is a phenomenon (event) involved in the task step of placing the terrarium plants in the planting medium. A study of this phenomenon might reveal "planting depth" as a critical property of "planting."

*Objects and/or procedures involved in doing each step.* As the phenomena and their critical properties are identified, they are listed on this part of the Project ILP format sheet. The same sources that were used for identifying the phenomena and critical properties probably also will be useful for learning about them.

Production Projects also have been called "carrier projects" because they "carry" learning. Teachers should be cautioned, however, not to expect projects to carry learning that is not specific to the achievement of the "product." Rather, when checking the student's list of objects and/or procedures involved in doing each step in the Production Project, the teacher should be concerned with questions such as the following: (1) Was the student able to carry out each task step adequately enough to achieve the specifications for the "product"? (2) Assuming that the task steps involved new competencies for the student, did the student correctly identify the phenomena involved in the new competencies? (3) As a result of his or her study, can the student identify the properties of the phenomena that are critical for the task steps involved?

For example, the richness of the potting soil obviously will have an effect on the growth rate of the terrarium plants. If the planting mixture is not rich enough, it may not support plant life. If it is too rich, the plants will grow spindly and thus defeat the purpose of a terrarium—which is to allow for slow, even growth. Assuming slow, uniform plant growth as one of the student's specifications for the terrarium project, what are the *critical* properties of the planting mix that the student must understand in order to control to the extent possible the growth rate of the plants?

Depending on the age and previous experience of the terrarium builder, information concerning planting mix might consist only of a knowledge of one or two reputable brands of commercial houseplant soil. For an older or more experienced student, it might consist of a knowledge of the general ingredients of terrarium soil (e.g., two parts fresh top soil, one part sand, one part compost, and some charcoal) so that the student might prepare his or her own mix. At another level, the student might be expected to know about and use the specific ingredients of high-grade potting soil (e.g., redwood leaf mold, oak leaf mold, peat moss, peat humus, forest humus, humusite, aqua-sorb, charcoal, perlite, and "sponge-rok"). Other learnings (e.g., the mineral composition, microbial activity, or colloidal complex of the soil), however interesting or peripherally related, would not be expected of most student terrarium builders at this point because this knowledge would not be *critical* to the successful completion of the project. Such learnings are in the category of "nice-to-know" but are not essential.

*Test.* A test generally is thought of as a terminal experience in any activity. However, we are using this heading in the Production Project format to remind the student and teacher of both en route progress checking and whatever evaluation activities are appropriate upon completion of the project.

Several stages in a Production Project ILP deserve formal progress checking by the teacher. These are points at which the student should be aware that he is responsible for obtaining teacher approval before continuing with the project. At least two progress checks probably are mandatory in any Production Project. These would occur (1) after the student has selected a "product" and stated the specifications, but before he has engaged in a task analysis, and (2) after the student has planned the production activity but before actually carrying out any of the project steps.

The first of these progress checks allows the teacher to help the student determine whether or not the planned project is within the response capabilities of the student and yet demanding enough to require new learnings. The second progress check, before actual production work begins, allows the teacher to examine the student's plans for completeness, for possible errors in planning, and for potentially hazardous activities. In addition, the second progress check allows the teacher to determine with the student (1) whether any additional progress checks will be required during or between any of the task steps and (2) whether the student will be required to secure a progress check from possible consultants to the project. Depending on the age and maturity of the terrarium builder, an obvious progress checkpoint might be immediately before the actual planting begins, particularly if student (or parent) expenditures have been involved.

When the "product" has been completed, evaluation takes place using the specifications that were recorded earlier. The teacher should be concerned with whether or not the student was able (1) to apply these specifications to his or her "product" and (2) to determine accurately the extent to which the "product" meets the specifications.

The Production Project "test" also may carry a more conventional meaning. The teacher may wish to determine the accuracy and extent of new concepts gained as a result of the project. Divergent forms of evaluation such as discussions or written reports may be used for this purpose. Convergent types of tests employing typical objective-type items also may be effective. The teacher may be well advised to use a relatively divergent evaluation approach if the Production Project is designed for "career education." On the other hand, the teacher in a vocational training program might prefer to use specific conceptual test items. The terrarium project example would lend itself to either procedure.

The "test" section of the Production Project design may be summarized in the following four statements:

(1)   The student will demonstrate his/her competence by performing each of the project steps that were identified.

(2)   The student will demonstrate his/her competence by comparing the final outcome of the project with the stated project specifications.

(3)   The student will discuss either orally or in writing what he/she has learned while doing the project.

(4)   The student will demonstrate mastery at the____% level or above of the conceptual content carried by the project.

*An example of a Production Project ILP.* Each of the six parts of the Production Project ILP format has been illustrated using various aspects of terrarium building. Using the same basic subject matter, Figure 5 contains a complete example of a teacher-designed Production Project ILP.

*Figure 5*

*Production Project ILP on Terrarium Building*

**Production Project ILP**

*"Product" (Goal):*     Terrarium (for a secondary level general science project)

*Specifications*:

Categories of specifications and examples of each are listed below. Depending on your prior background, you first may need to examine the broad topic of "terrariums" and then decide on your specifications.

(1)     Terrarium type (e.g., desert, field or wood, bog or swamp, semi-aquatic, etc.).

(2)     Container type (e.g., glass or plastic, wide top, aquarium type, brandy snifter, glass bubble, dome, narrow-neck, etc.).

(3)     Compatibility characteristics (e.g., of plants with each other, of plants with container, of terrarium type with anticipated location, of container size with anticipated surrounding furniture and decor, etc.).

(4)     Aesthetic properties (e.g., soil terrain; plant blend, texture, color, shape, size, leaf pattern, and arrangement; "interest centers" such as figures and colored stones; etc.).

(5)     Etc.

*Steps You Will Follow*:

The steps you will follow may be grouped under the three main categories listed below. Examples of possible initial steps for each category are provided to help you get started on your task analysis.

*(Continued)*

*Figure 5 (Continued)*

(1) Preparatory steps
   (a) Select a container and plants.
   (b) Gather materials (e.g., planting tools, planting media, etc.).
   (c) Set up a work area and cover it with paper or plastic.
   (d) Experiment with possible plant arrangements outside of the container.
   (e) Etc.

(2) Planting steps
   (a) Place the planting media in appropriate layers in the container.
   (b) Prepare the soil bed in the desired terrain.
   (c) Prepare holes for the plants.
   (d) Etc.

(3) Finishing touches
   (a) Place "added attractions" (figures, stones, bark, moss, etc.) in the terrarium.
   (b) Clean the stray bits of soil, etc., from the inside surface of the container and polish the outside surface.
   (c) Provide an initial watering (this is a crucial step).
   (d) Etc.

*Where You Could Learn About Each Step*:

(1) Visit a nursery (after making prior arrangements to observe terrariums being constructed).
(2) Obtain audiovisual media, articles, books, worksheets, and self-tests on terrariums. These are available both in the school media center and in the public library. Also useful are specialized reference books such as *The Book of Popular Science* and general encyclo-

*(Continued)*

## *Figure 5 (Continued)*

pedias such as *World Book Encyclopedia* and *Encyclopedia Americana.*

(3)   Examine general science textbooks, which occasion-
ally contain sections on terrariums.

(4)   Visit a local botanical garden.

(5)   Attend a regular meeting of a local horticultural
society.

(6)   A parent, relative, or friend who is an expert on
terrariums may be known to someone in the class or
school. Check around. Perhaps this person might be
willing to serve as a consultant for the terrarium
Production Project.

(7)   Etc.

*Objects and/or Procedures Involved
in Doing Each Step*:

Some of the phenomena that may be involved in the
construction, placement, and care of your terrarium are the
following:

(1)   Diseases
    (a)   Fungus
    (b)   Insect

(2)   Heat
    (a)   Absorption
    (b)   Entrapment
    (c)   Radiation

(3)   Humidity

(4)   Light
    (a)   Etiolation
    (b)   Photochemical
        equivalence

        (i)   Light
             endurance
        (ii)  Light
             intensity
    (c)   Photosynthesis
    (d)   Phototropism

(5)   Planting
    (a)   Depth
    (b)   Procedures
    (c)   Root care
    (d)   Rooting hormone

(6)   Plants
    (a)   Identity

*(Continued)*

*Figure 5 (Continued)*

(b) Health
(c) Environmental requirements
(d) Purchased
(e) Collected

(7) Soil
   (a) Composition
   (b) Function
      (i) Air
      (ii) Anchorage
      (iii) Food — organic, chemical
      (iv) Water
   (c) Sterilization
   (d) Testing

(8) Tools

(a) Cleaner
(b) Duster
(c) Funnel
(d) Placer
(e) Pruner
(f) Shovel
(g) Soil tester
(h) Tamper
(i) Tweezer
(j) Watering device

(9) Watering requirements
   (a) Constantly moist
   (b) Surface dry
   (c) Below surface dry
   (d) Drench and dry

(10) Etc.

*Test*:

(1) Your terrarium will be evaluated on the basis of the specifications that you developed and that were accepted by your teacher.
(2) You will be asked to participate (a) in a conference with your teacher or (b) in a small group discussion that also may include other students who have completed similar projects. In either case, you should be prepared to communicate about the phenomena listed above and/or any others that you may have studied in order to complete your terrarium project. The levels of cognition that you should be prepared to demonstrate with respect to the phenomena involved in terrariums include "knowledge," "comprehension," and "application."
(3) You may be asked to share your newly acquired skills and knowledge by demonstrating terrarium building to a class not currently studying the topic or to a community group or club.

Terrarium construction as it might occur in a junior high or high school general science class is shown in Figure 5.

### Project ILPs and Teacher Roles

Teacher roles have been alluded to throughout the preceding discussion of Project ILP design formats. In this section we will concentrate on the teacher's role in helping students to *self*-evaluate their Issue and Production Project activities and outcomes.

Student self-evaluation is a very important part of life-based educational programs. The student should reflect both on the *processes* he has used and on the *products* he has produced. The following are several student self-evaluation questions that get at the processes involved in Issue Project ILPs:

(1) Did I identify the issue accurately so that it fits in the form, "What should be done about ... ?" Did I clearly name the phenomenon that is the focus of the issue?

(2) Was I able to respond to the question, "What am I trying to gain or to protect for myself and for others?" in such a way that clearly demonstrated the issue's impact on my own values and on the values of others?

(3) Have I identified the values that I want to maximize and those that I want to minimize?

(4) Was I able to identify alternative ways of resolving the issue? Was creativity a factor?

(5) Was I able to respond to the following questions concerning each of the alternative resolutions for the issue:
(a) What is involved in carrying it out?
(b) What are its probable consequences for myself and others?

(6) Did I resolve the issue by actually choosing an alternative?

(7)  Am I able to justify my choice after having examined inconsistencies that may have been revealed in my own beliefs? Am I able to justify my choice after having weighed the alternatives in terms of the net effect on my own and others' values?

The "product" making processes required in Production Project ILPs may be self-evaluated by students through use of questions such as the following:

(1)  Did I name the "product" accurately?

(2)  Were the specifications that I developed for the "product" adequate both for guiding its production and for evaluating its final form?

(3)  Did my task analysis result in the actual steps that I carried out in producing the "product," or did I need to expand or in some other way modify the steps while the project was in progress?

(4)  Did I list all of the materials and equipment that were needed to complete the project?

(5)  Was I able to identify within each step the content to be learned in order to carry out that step competently?

(6)  Did I carry out the planned learning activities?

(7)  Did I obtain appropriate consultant help by taking advantage of the progress checks identified in my Production Project ILP?

(8)  Did I complete the project?

(9)  Did the final "product" meet specifications?

At some point during the student self-evaluation process, the student also should have the opportunity to reflect on the *feelings* that resulted from the issue resolving and "product" making activities. The following questions are useful for this purpose:

(1) Did I choose the issue or the "product" for the Project ILP or did someone else choose it for me? In either case, was I committed to this project?

(2) Was the project interesting for me, or was it dull?

(3) Were the plans that I made for carrying out the project realistic?

(4) What amount of effort did I expend? Great? Modest? Small?

(5) Did I learn anything that I did not already know? Very much? Some? None?

(6) Was I satisfied with the resolution of the issue or with the "product" that resulted from my project?

To conclude, the role of the teacher as a facilitator of student self-evaluation rather than as the sole judge of the student's work may be somewhat unfamiliar to many teachers. The development of such teacher skills is worthwhile, however. Because of the direct relationship between Project ILPs and in-life tasks, the rewards for learners of skillful self-evaluation are substantial.

## References
### *(DESIGN FORMAT section)*

Kapfer, P.G. Educational Technology and Individualized Teaching in Higher Education. Paper presented at the Second Brazilian National Conference of Educational Technology Applied to Higher Education (II CONTECE), Sao Paulo, Brazil, October, 1973.

Kapfer, P.G. and M.B. Kapfer. *What's the Score? A Teacher's Guide to LIM Record-Keeping Systems.* Salt Lake City, Utah: Bureau of Educational Research, University of Utah, 1975.

Woodruff, A.D. *The Life-Involvement Model of Education (LIM): A System Description.* Salt Lake City, Utah: Bureau of Educational Research, University of Utah, 1973.

Woodruff, A.D. The Goals and Critical features of a LIM Educational Program: A Succinct Statement. Salt Lake City, Utah: Bureau of Educational Research, University of Utah, 1974.

# IV.

# OUTCOMES

The outcomes for students of using Project ILPs may be thought of as both primary and secondary in nature. Primary outcomes include both the processes of learning that are employed and the content that is the focus of these processes. Secondary outcomes may consist of a variety of independency and creativity factors, such as self-initiative, self-direction, dependability, and spontaneity. Other such outcomes might include the generation of numerous and uncommon alternatives to issues or the completion of creative or extraordinary "products."

Too little adherence to the details of implementing the Project ILP instructional designs may result in indefensible issue resolving, sloppy "products," and few if any measurable primary or secondary outcomes. Because people learn what they practice, the Project ILP instructional designs should be implemented very explicitly *as to their intent* so that the primary outcomes are literally practiced. In addition, student practice of the learning processes should be designed to promote desired secondary outcomes. For example, creativity outcomes may be built into Project ILPs and, thus, creativity may be provided for *directly* rather than as an alternative to structure, clarity, and thoughtfulness.

**Outcomes for the Student**

Primary and secondary outcomes from the use of Project

ILPs may occur in the following three areas: (1) proficiency outcomes, (2) confidence outcomes, and (3) commitment outcomes. The curricular content for the first of these has been discussed in earlier sections of this book and includes both processes and phenomena. In the Project ILP designs, we have not identified curricular content as such for the second and third outcomes. Rather, confidence and commitment outcomes are the direct result of *how* proficiency outcomes are attained and are only indirectly related to *which* proficiencies are achieved.

*Proficiency outcomes.* Most would agree that the ultimate test of a proficiency's value, i.e., the value of knowledge and/or skill, is in the degree to which it improves the life of its possessor (Seeley, 1969). This is the core outcome anticipated from the use of Project ILPs. Life-based educational programs engage students in projects that are purposeful for students at the time that they are done rather than at some vague, future time and circumstance.

A number of process proficiencies are anticipated at the day-to-day level of instruction that are judged to be essential to successful living. Students recognize issues in their daily lives that are worth resolving and "products" that they would like to obtain or create. Students become proficient in rational processes for coping with issues. The performance of the issue resolution steps is at a level of quality that consistently results in the choice of personally valued goals. As a result of achieving a large number and variety of valued goals, students gain proficiency in "product" making processes. They learn to make sound operational decisions concerning the use of resources while engaged in the pursuit of their goals. They learn to make efficient and reliable decisions concerning the attainment and use of the instrumental abilities needed for that pursuit. Students communicate effectively about ideas, feelings, and actions. Such communication is in evidence throughout and at the conclusion of issue resolving and "product" making activities.

While engaged in Project ILPs, students are practicing what people do in their everyday lives and while on the job. The examples of issues and "products" used for illustrative purposes throughout this book provide ample data to document this statement. To the extent that Project ILPs are carried out under conditions that match life-based performance of these same activities, one might anticipate familiarities and proficiencies in various careers and vocations. Life style familiarity may be achieved when students go into the community to carry out their Project ILPs in real-life settings. The important point concerning career-related outcomes from the use of Project ILPs is that the *potential* is inherent in the approach, but such outcomes should not be left to chance. The concept of the school as a foyer to the community is a useful one in this regard. Implications for teacher and administrator roles in establishing and maintaining contact with community resources will be discussed later.

*Confidence outcomes.* Project ILPs are carefully designed to maximize the probability of student success in meaningful tasks. Project ILPs contribute to the student's increased control of his or her own environment. Through personal choice of valued goals and well-planned actions for achieving those goals, the student learns how environmental things respond, and hopefully, how to anticipate those responses for increasingly successful choices of "ends" and "means." Careful planning includes both identification of the steps to be performed in issue resolution and "product" making, and identification of and provision for any new learning that must be accomplished. Thus, sound planning may be thought of both as a prerequisite for and as an outcome of confidence.

Project ILPs carried out under life-based conditions contribute to confidence outcomes that are particularly important from societal points of view. For example, students who gain confidence in their ability to earn a living in a number of different but potentially rewarding occupations are better equipped for dealing with necessary job changes that may result from schooling, family, or other responsibilities. Other societally important confidence outcomes may be anticipated when periodic Project ILPs deal specifically with the phenomena involved in human relationships, roles, and arrangements.

*Commitment outcomes.* Commitment outcomes are seen whenever a student obligates himself by personal choice to a course of action. Verbalization about the commitment and about the actions, and the carrying out of the actions themselves, are the observable indicators of commitment. Commitment is not something that is "taught." Rather, the teacher creates conditions that expose the student to interesting phenomena, to potentially attractive goals, and to meaningful issues so that the student may change his or her own motivational state.

Commitment outcomes are the direct product of rationally chosen goals. The Issue Project ILP is a formal design for promoting such rational choices. The student's careful analysis of his or her personal values, as an integral part of the resolution process, is intended to assure student commitment to the choice made. Commitment outcomes also are anticipated from student opportunities to choose their own "products" for formulation.

Voluntary student commitment to tasks is an ideal toward which many teachers strive (1) by offering broad tasks that may be delimited on the basis of student interests, and (2) by offering alternative tasks. Project ILPs lend themselves readily to this general pattern. Such healthy flexibility bears directly on the question of "standards," however. If a community values highly the development of student commitment that results in responsible, purposeful, meaningful, goal-directed behavior, then the community must consider granting an appropriate degree of flexibility to the school as to when and how educational standards are to be met.

### Outcomes for the Teacher and Administrator

An important outcome of the ILP approach for teachers is the change in role from that of information transmitter to that of student-task facilitator. Most school staffs have very little difficulty with this as an abstract idea. Operationalizing the idea, as shown in Figure 6 (Kapfer, Kapfer, Woodruff, and Stutz, 1970), involves two principal categories of teacher actions. First, the teacher is responsible for providing or approving topics and tasks for Project ILPs. Second, the teacher is responsible for stimulating and monitoring student participation in the learning activities. The enjoyable teacher's role of "telling" may sometimes shift the educative interaction focus to a position between the learner and the teacher rather than keeping it where it should be—between the learner and the task. As a result, memorization of information may replace the rich concept-forming experiences that should be the basis for such memory work.

Teacher-student interactions *other* than teacher "telling" are especially appropriate when using Project ILPs. The teacher who asks, "What will happen if one of the four engines of your rocket does not fire?" is focusing the student's attention on the task, not on the teacher. This one-to-one role of the teacher, given typical class sizes, usually is possible only as a trade-off from other time-consuming tasks. For example, excessive "telling" uses up time that otherwise might be devoted to promoting student-task interaction. Likewise, too much testing of verbal information not only consumes teacher and student time, but

*Figure 6*

*Student-Task Interaction*

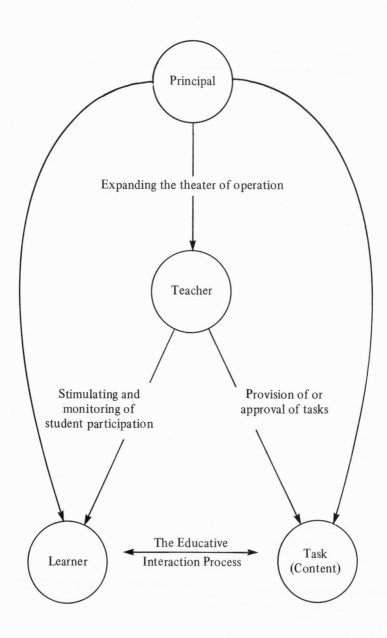

also removes from the student the responsibility for self-evaluation.

In a school using Project ILPs, the primary roles of the principal include (1) expanding teacher access to resources and locations for students to engage in life-based Project ILPs, (2) crediting teachers for creating the conditions that are necessary for the learner-task interaction process to take place, and (3) expanding teacher and community ideas about the curriculum.

To use an analogy, the function of instructional designs, content, and resources in schools may be somewhat like the planting requirements of several varieties of seed. Some educators and communities may plant only one type of academic "seed," or they may identify only one method of planting—often "blanket" coverage or "broadcast" seeding. For example, teacher-selected content may be uniformly "covered" irrespective of student interests, purposes, and needs. Farmers know that alternative methods of planting, such as in checkrows, hills, or continuous rows, may be usefully matched to seed types, soil composition, climate conditions, or desired yields. In somewhat the same way, instructional designs may be matched to the student's chosen learning tasks. New educational ideas, like new varieties of seed, have their antecedents in older varieties. The principal differences may be in how they are cultivated, in the systematics of their use, or in the kind of adversity for which they have built-in resistance. The administrator's job is to sort out the most promising components of this mix for the unique conditions in his or her school and community.

## References
### (OUTCOMES section)

Kapfer, P.G., M.B. Kapfer, A.D. Woodruff, and R.C. Stutz.

*Toward the Life-Internship Curriculum.* Carson City, Nevada: Nevada State Department of Education, 1970, p. 47.

Seeley, J.R. Some Skills of Being for Those in Service in Education. *Life Skills in Schools and Society*, L.J. Rubin (Ed.). Washington, D.C.: Association for Supervision and Curriculum Development, 1969, p. 128.

# V.

# DEVELOPMENTAL GUIDE

This section is intended to be a procedural guide for the teacher for operationalizing the Project ILP instructional designs in the classroom. Such a procedural guide is different, of course, from a "how-to-write-an-ILP" guide. Although information of the "how to" variety will be included, this section will focus on ideas about steps the teacher may take to introduce teacher-constructed Project ILPs and to set the stage for students to self-initiate and self-construct their own ILPs. The rather pervasive classroom organizational and attitudinal changes that may be required for a shift to Project ILPs will be mentioned also. Our purpose is to suggest ways to get *some* Project ILPs into the classroom. The creative teacher will take it from there.

**Content Index**

The teacher's first step is to informally assess the content in his or her area of teaching responsibility. What are the possibilities for Project ILPs? Are there any obvious issues or "products" that would capture student interest? Depending on the age of the students and the degree of curricular freedom that is available in the system, it might be useful to begin by trying out with selected students a small number of potential issue topics and "product" ideas. The teacher might then enlist the help of such students in developing an index

of potential issues and "products" that students at that age level would relate to easily. It may be well to keep in mind that the teacher's objective at this stage is relatively modest— the construction of a simple index for tryout purposes. Completeness of the index is not necessary until Project ILPs are expected to "carry" a major portion of the learning load of a course or classroom. A more complete index and other support systems may be added as needed.

### Course Requirements

As long as curricula are organized by subjects and grades, teachers must be concerned about course requirements within these two basic kinds of organizational patterns. Given the restrictive reality that this logical but not life-based compartmentalization affords, much still can be accomplished. For example, it appears that both kinds of Project ILPs have a place at every grade level and in virtually every subject area. This is the case because issue resolving and "product" making *in life* involve phenomena from all kinds of "school content" areas. As a bonus, of course, students gain practice in the systematic procedures for issue resolving and "product" making.

Now, let us free ourselves of grade-level and conventional subject area constraints and, without creating some other administrative structure, look at "requirements" from a psychological point of view. In order to progress from immaturity to maturity in a given action, the number of phenomena and/or the complexity of the phenomena may be increased incrementally. For example, in the action of "calculating," operations such as adding, subtracting, multiplying, and dividing are phenomena of varying complexity that may become involved. The adding of other phenomena such as fractions, decimals, and exponential notation gradually increases the complexity of the total act of calculating.

This same line of development may be applied to any action in order to identify the content that may be required for whatever level of maturity is expected for that action.

This approach to curricular organization, therefore, may be thought of as a two-dimensional grid. The horizontal line might be used for identifying required and optional actions. For each action, the vertical line might be used for identifying required and optional phenomena. Any given action, such as calculating, singing, diagnosing, skiing, or drawing, may be on-going even before a child enters school. The school's responsibility, then, is to encourage (1) continuation of already on-going actions, (2) start-up of new actions, and (3) addition of phenomena to mature both of these.

## Community Resources and Learning Stations

Many elementary schools are lacking in common household appliances, hand tools, and appropriate work stations. This may make some Project ILPs difficult to accomplish without considerable parental cooperation. At the secondary and post-secondary levels this situation improves considerably with the addition of laboratories, shops, business machines, family living centers, and the like. Even so, the basic problem with conventional school resources is that students are capable of dealing with much more than is typically available in school settings. As a result, teachers and students need access to selected community resources, including the talent of the people who normally use these resources. One useful way of obtaining such information is the Keysort card presented in Figure 7. Using such a device, an individual teacher or school can survey parents and others for potential talent and resources.

## Introducing Project ILPs

As indicated earlier, both kinds of Project ILPs embody

*Figure 7*

*Identifying Parent and Community Resources for Learning
(Reprinted with permission of the Murray City
School District, Murray, Utah)*

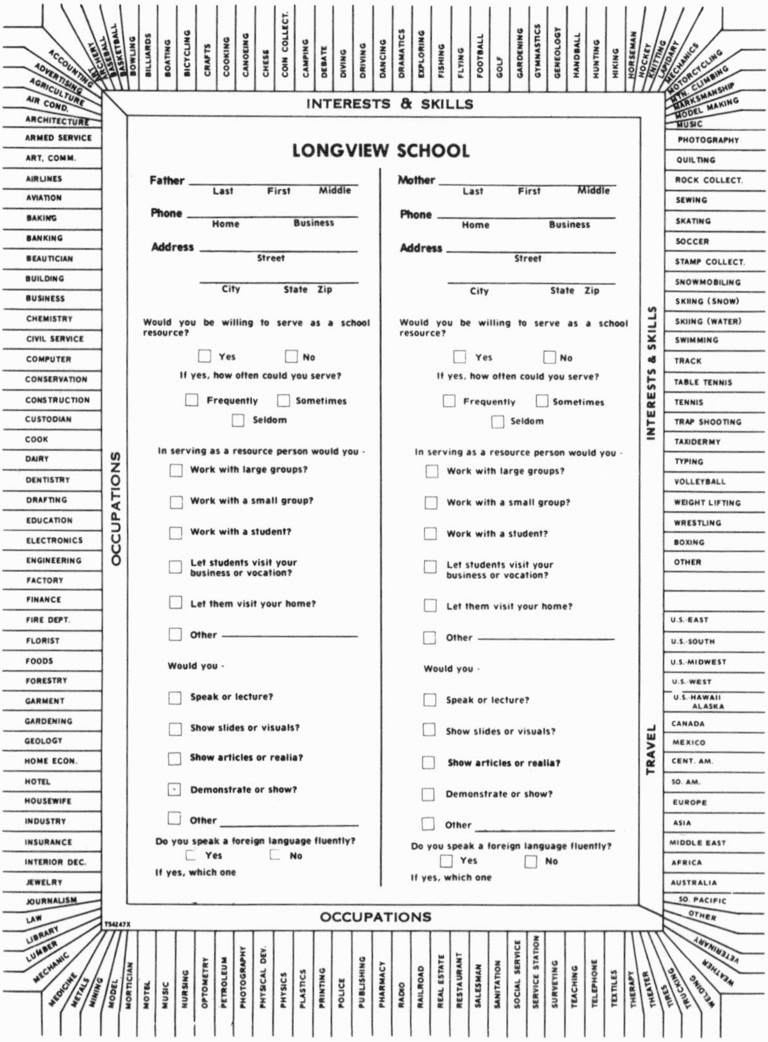

processes that people already employ to a greater or lesser extent in their out-of-school lives. This fact should be taken into account in planning the approach to introducing students to the two Project ILP instructional designs. Tryout of the designs with a few selected students, as mentioned earlier, probably is an ideal way to start. Such students can help by subsequently teaming with other students as the use of Project ILPs is expanded to an entire classroom. Experienced students also can help in the formulation of the teacher's plan for an introductory total-class project.

**Recording Life-Based Outcomes**

Simple record-keeping systems that can be kept by the students themselves with monitoring by the teacher are particularly useful. In addition, student self-evaluation techniques may be built directly into the records to encourage development in this important area. Record-keeping systems also may be designed to facilitate monitoring the adequacy of subject matter coverage (perhaps through a check-off listing of content categories) and the development of personal goal-setting ability (through periodic listing of intermediate and long-range student goals). Obviously, school records also should serve to credit student accomplishment. Such record-keeping systems assume a shift in values away from the role of the teacher as a judge and toward the complementary roles of teacher and student as responsible partners in the learning endeavor.

**Summary**

The development and use of Project ILPs, like nearly any other systematic instructional approach, require the time, talent, and effort of dedicated teachers and supportive administrators. When properly introduced and implemented, the student enjoys the independence of action and variety of content that are available through Project ILPs. Both teachers and administrators are gratified when student enthusiasm for learning results in pleased parents. In the last analysis, however, school is a place for learning. Project ILPs are an effective device for "carrying" learning in such a way that its importance and meaningfulness are perceived by the student.

# VI.

# RESOURCES

Project ILPs are an ideal way or organizing learning activities and resources for the resolution of life-based issues, for planning ways of obtaining life-based "products," and for securing the knowledge and skill needed for both of these kinds of activities. The two types of Project ILPs presented in this book have been under development for nearly a decade. Descriptive information related to the theory and use of Project ILP instructional designs is available from the following published sources (unpublished and in-house sources cited earlier are not repeated here):

## BOOKS

Kapfer, Philip G. and Miriam Bierbaum Kapfer. *Inquiry ILPs: Individualized Learning Plans for Life-Based Inquiry* (Instructional Design Library). Englewood Cliffs, New Jersey: Educational Technology Publications, Inc., 1978. 75 pp.

Kapfer, Philip G. and Miriam Bierbaum Kapfer (Eds.). *Learning Packages in American Education.* Englewood Cliffs, New Jersey: Educational Technology Publications, Inc., 1972. 233 pp.

Kapfer, Philip G., Miriam Bierbaum Kapfer, Asahel D. Woodruff, and Rowan C. Stutz. *Toward the Life-Internship Curriculum.* Carson City, Nevada: Nevada State Department of Education, 1970. 68 pp.

Kapfer, Philip G. and Glen F. Ovard. *Preparing and Using Individualized Learning Packages for Ungraded, Continuous Progress Education.* Englewood Cliffs, New Jersey: Educational Technology Publications, Inc., 1971. 264 pp.

## ARTICLES

Kapfer, Philip G. A Humanistic Theory of Individualized Instruction. *THRUST—for Educational Leadership* (Journal of the Association of California School Administrators), May 1975, *4*, 5-7.

Kapfer, Philip G. An Instructional Management Strategy for Individualizing Learning. *Phi Delta Kappan*, January 1968, *49*, 260-263.

Kapfer, Philip G. Practical Approaches to Individualizing Instruction. *Educational Screen and Audiovisual Guide*, May 1968, *47*, 14-16.

Kapfer, Philip G. and Miriam Bierbaum Kapfer. Introduction to Learning Packages. *Educational Technology*, September 1972, *12*, 9-11.

Kapfer, Philip G., Miriam Bierbaum Kapfer, and Asahel D. Woodruff. Declining Test Scores: Interpretations, Issues and Relationship to Life-Based Education. *Educational Technology*, July 1976, *16*, 5-12.

Kapfer, Philip G., Miriam Bierbaum Kapfer, Asahel D. Woodruff, and Rowan C. Stutz. Realism and Relevance—Payoffs of the Life-Internship Approach. *Educational Technology*, November 1970, *10*, 29-31.

Kapfer, Philip G. and Gardner Swenson. Individualizing Instruction for Self-Paced Learning. *The Clearing House*, March 1968, *42*, 405-410.

Kapfer, Philip G. and William H. Wallin. PACE for Change. *Nevada Education*, Spring 1968, *3*, 8-9 and 28-29.

Kapfer, Philip G. and Asahel D. Woodruff. The Life-Involvement Model of Curriculum and Instruction. *Educational Technology*, September 1972, *12*, 64-72.

Smith, Lucille W. and Philip G. Kapfer. Classroom Management of Learning Package Programs. *Educational Technology*, September 1972, *12*, 80-85.

Woodruff, Asahel D. A Behavior-Oriented Curriculum Model. *Behavioral Emphasis in Art Education*, ed. D. Jack Davis. Reston, Virginia: National Art Education Association, 1975, pp. 13-41.

Woodruff, Asahel D. The Rationale. *Theory Into Practice*, December 1968, 7, 197-202.

Woodruff, Asahel D. and Philip G. Kapfer. Behavioral Objectives and Humanism in Education: A Question of Specificity. *Educational Technology*, January 1972, *12*, 51-55.

## WORKSHOP

The authors conduct a two-day workshop on ILP approaches.

PHILIP G. KAPFER holds a dual appointment as Research Professor in the Department of Education, Graduate School of Education, and in the Spencer S. Eccles Health Sciences Library at the University of Utah. His divided assignment includes the development of curricular and instructional designs in the public schools and in the health sciences colleges at the University. In addition, Dr. Kapfer serves as Head of the Learning Resource Center at Eccles Library and is a staff member in the Bureau of Educational Research. His current interests are centered on life-based educational programs and the use of computer-assisted instruction. Formerly a chemistry, physics, and mathematics teacher, Dr. Kapfer worked for five years with elementary and secondary teachers in the Clark County School District, Las Vegas, Nevada, on individualization strategies for public school classrooms. He has been a faculty member at the University of Utah since 1970. Dr. Kapfer has published numerous articles and three books and has conducted many workshops on instructional design.

MIRIAM BIERBAUM KAPFER is Research Professor in the Department of Special Education and is on the staff of the bureau of Educational Research, Graduate School of Education, University of Utah. She is Co-Director of the Life-Involvement Model, and is closely involved with the development of innovative educational programs in the public schools. Her current interests also include instructional designs for exceptional children and the arts. Dr. Kapfer is an expert on the use of behavioral objectives in curriculum development, having edited a book on that topic in 1971. Formerly a music and English teacher at the elementary and secondary levels, Dr. Kapfer also worked as Research Specialist in the Clark County School District, Las Vegas, Nevada, prior to coming to the University of Utah. Dr. Kapfer has published many articles and three books on various aspects of the broad field of educational planning.